From My
Facebook Friends

To all people needing reminders
that fresh perspectives
from candid people exist.

From My Facebook Friends

Compiled By
Mylia Tiye Mal Jaza

Cover Design By
Muhammad Asad
of Photo_Arena

Proofread By
Sun Child Wind Spirit

Edited By
Dr. Mari Michelle

BePublished.Org

Be Published

From My Facebook Friends

First Edition. Printed In the USA.
Recycled Paper Encouraged.

ISBN-10: 1545121826
ISBN-13: 978-1545121826

Author
Mylia Tiye Mal Jaza
GoddessSage@bepublished.biz
www.myliajaza.gqnu.net

Self-Publishing Associate
Mary M. Jefferson
BePublished.Org - Chicago
(972) 880-8316
www.bepublished.org
www.maryjefferson.us
mari@bepublished.org

Imprint of Record
CreateSpace On-Demand Publishing
7290-B Investment Drive
Charleston, SC 29418

Table of Posts

SCREENSHOTS

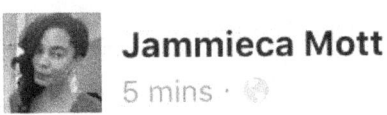

Jammieca Mott
5 mins ·

Preparation begets opportunity.

 **Daryl Courtney** is feeling determined.

1 min ·

Speak into your atmosphere! Regardless of your situation or circumstance! Refocus and declare that all things work together for the good to them that love God! Remember you are here on purpose! Speak It! And trust the process! He that shall come will come! God bless

 **Jeffrey Burns**
29 mins ·

Beautiful it is so hard to love you with your tall armor of pride , something that you feel you need to have so you can be perceived as strong.so tall that I can't even see who you truly are. !!!

 **Delores Jones** is 😊 feeling amused.
1 hr · Prairie Village, KS · 🌐

So, recently a guy asked me out to dinner. I accepted the invitation and enjoyed the experience. Several weeks went by and I didn't hear from him. I was perfectly find with that. Well, on yesterday, I received a text from him stating, "You must have forgotten about me." I replied, "well, now, when you are a no call and no show, you lose your job." Lol. I'm just stating the facts. Remember ladies, you must check his trash, his treasure and his track record. Gentleman, don't forget that the most attractive thing to a woman about a man is "consistency." Case closed. Lol.

Donald Shaffer
February 7 at 1:42pm · 🌐

Is it just me, or does it seem as though President Trump's cabinet nominees are either woefully unqualified or people with a history of hostility toward the very departments they will lead (eg. Ben Carson will lead HUD, but he has actually said that he believes "poverty is a choice;" Scott Pruitt, his nod for EPA Secretary, has made a career of suing the EPA for what he believes is the agency's overreach in protecting the environment against business interests). And NOW, quite possibly the most unqualified person in the history of Presidential Cabinet nominations, Betsy DeVos will head the Department of Education. This is a woman who said that the threat of Grizzly Bears necessitates the presence of guns in a particular school district; in what world of "alternative facts" is this not a disqualifying statement? So it appears clear what is happening; Republicans have long wanted to strip down the Federal Government, thereby rendering it incapable of regulating big business or leveling the playing field for the most vulnerable Americans. Trump is their all-too-willing puppet; so his strategy of undermining these agencies from within serves their interests perhaps better than any Republican President to date. That his nominees are not just in ideological lock step with Republican/Conservative thinking but also entirely unqualified as well, is even better. It means they can't do a good job even if they tried. So the inevitable public outcry when our public education system is gutted, when teacher unions are quashed, when public parks and public lands are sold off, when the Clean Air and Water Acts are no longer strictly enforced, when it becomes more difficult for middle class people to own a home, ALL of these concerns will be met with either indifference or incompetence. Get ready America; our way of life is about to change. I suggest everyone study up on "Social Darwinism" and read every Ayn Rand novel. Got to be prepared for this "Brave New World."

 **Malika Rasheedah**
42 mins · 🌐

What he said 😅😄🤗

 **Twan Blackgate**
1 hr · 👥

I'VE LEARNED WITH INDEPENDENT
WOMEN YOU JUST HAVE TO DO FOR
THEM WITHOUT ASKING THEM DO
THEY NEED HELP BECAUSE MANY
AREN'T GOING TO ASK YOU FOR
ANYTHING. THEIR PRIDE WON'T LET
THEM. SO YOU JUST HAVE TO SEE A
BILL SHE HAS LAYING AROUND AND
RANDOMLY PAY IT... GRAB HER KEYS
AND JUST FILL HER TANK W GAS AND
GET HER CAR WASHED... JUST
SIMPLE THINGS. AM I LYING?

Montré Bible
52 mins · Dallas, TX ·

I wanna sexy body but I love whataburger Soooo muuuuch...

Mar Quel
Yesterday at 2:40pm ·

Shots out to my Sugar Momma... I like random gifts

 **MsSmiley Davis**

1 hr ·

, Why do fools fall nluv ' an jus b there? Sum 1 please tell me

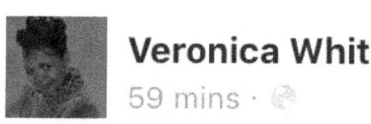

Veronica Whitby
59 mins ·

whatever the problem or situation may be....#GodisBIGGER

Don Wansley
5 mins ·

The war is not of countries,
but of light and dark. Energy

 **Zukeeya Moore**
5 hrs ·

You can't trust a TOO SAVED person. They can be just as messy!

 **Stafon Harris-Jackson** was 😊 feeling confident at 📍 **Texas Health (Arlington, TX)**.

9 hrs · Arlington, TX · 🌐

Getting ready to learn all about living and understanding Diabetes one day at a time. I'm confident that I can do this. #life #staypositive

 **Erica Edwards**

March 16 at 8:29am · 🌐

Believe you will succeed! You have three of the most important traits for success: hardworking, knowing what you don't know, and asking for help. #growth

Shawn Lane
January 20 · 🌐

This is the day that the Lord has made, I'm rejoicing and I'm glad in it!

 **Mickey Simmons**
16 hrs ·

It's not natural beauty if you letting make up control your face.

 **Mickey Simmons**
4 hrs ·

Prove to yourself that you are a better person. Never try to prove it to anyone else. As long as you know your personal growth. No one else can change that.
#growth

Neek Walker
3 hrs ·

Moving on and starting a new life journey is great for anybody.... But when you leave, stiff your Kids Mom with your bills, lie to your kids about buying them clothes, running out the house like a thief in the middle of the night....thats simply called being a coward.Have a great life... Cause I will enjoy mine. Ase' the long way.

25

 **Monique Davis**
20 hrs ·

Working on a personalized sketch for a dear
friend. This is a snapshot of my process.
Practice, practice, practice.

 **Christopher D Madden**
5 mins · 🌐

Never let people who were too scared to Jump to tell you why you shouldn't. Go BIG! Sometimes your vision will scare you but intimidate them. Get off the Shore and go for MORE!!!! #FREEDOMINGISCOMING

WorkHorse Williams

3 hrs · 🌐

Note to Self!!
Never settle, Never be
Satisfied!!! &
Stay out of MY Way!!!

 **Jacqueline Denise**
2 hrs ·

I have a designation already designed for my destiny!

Erick Snyder
1 hr · South Tampa, FL · 👥

People would treat people different if they put themselves in their position.

 **LaTonia Jefferson Lewis** shared
Pastor Jamal Bryant's **post**.
2 hrs ·

 Pastor Jamal Bryant
16 hrs ·

When you are a threat....you will always be
a target

Tony Hunt Dunmore is  feeling perplexed.

1 hr ·

I'm sitting back looking at these people that I thought were older than me. To find out how wrong I was. Looking like something just pulled them out the grave last night. I have to wonder how many hard lives have you lived? I can't laugh at them, I am and feel tired, but if I can get rid of these bags under my eyes I would be straight

 **Jay Tillman**
13 mins ·

Food for thought ...If you light a lamp for someone else it will also brighten your path.

 **DeMarquis Clarke** at ♀ **Mount Ararat Baptist Church.**

Yesterday at 8:23am · Pittsburgh, PA · 🔒

I'm in the parking lot about to go into church and thought back to a conversation I recently had with my mom. My mom and I were talking about a big decision I need to make, when half way through the conversation (like during most of our conversations) God came up.

Me: Well, I am going to put this decision in the Lord's hands like I do with all the major decisions in my life, and be still so I can listen to him guide me.

My mom: Silence

(I think she's been questioning my relationship with God, so I went on to say...)

Me: Yeah mom, just because I haven't gone to church in the 8 years I've been in Pittsburgh doesn't mean I don't have a loving, connected relationship with God. It means that I refuse to endure humans' hatred, bigotry and homophobia in a place that I need to be experiencing God's love. I spent way too much time enduring that growing up and I refuse to endure it in adulthood.

My mom: I understand...

So, I am not sure about next Sunday or the Sunday after that, but on this Sunday, I decided to take the chance and experience God's love in his house. #prayforme 😪 🙏 🤍

Reginald Hathorn
2 hrs ·

When you grow and evolve, you run the risk of growing beyond people and places you love...TAKE THE RISK

#itsworththerisk #itsoktogrow #alwaysevolve

Luvn Lyfe
3 hrs ·

FAITH comes by HEARING and HEARING by THE WORD OF GOD...notice it didn't say faith comes by seeing. Faith has the power to change what you see...hearing the Word of God has the POWER to change what you see!!!! LET FAITH ARISE!!!!!

Vernon Moore
4 hrs ·

Today will be the best day of your life!!! #HappyMonday #MakeItAGreatDay!

Bro Reginald Hendrix
52 mins ·

The SUBconscious mind is a most powerful force in your life. Much of what we experience in life starts in the mind and becomes your physical reality manifest. Let us be careful if what we feed our subconscious mind (Music, tv shows, images etc.) because we may be Manifesting something in our SUBconscious that we don't want. Protect yourselves people. There's a war out here. Love 💘

Ephesians 6:12
"For we wrestle not against flesh and blood, but against principalities, against powers, against the rulers of the darkness of this world, against spiritual wickedness in high places."

Steamfunkateers! Some of y'all are wondering, 'what happened to Menna after From Here to Timbuktu?' Here's a hint of things to come...

Famara dismounted his camel a good distance away from the akedamel's tent. The guards immediately searched him, removing his guns and knives. They signaled him forward and he was escorted to the tent. Guards flanking the tent flap raised it for him to enter. He ducked his head then entered. The insides were sparse, befitting the person who now ruled the entire expanse known to the Ihaagaren as Tinariwen

The lone figure standing before him wore a white outfit, a rifle hanging from the shoulder. She turned to face him, a slight smile on her umber face. When they first met years ago her face was covered. Seeing her stern beauty for the first time, Famara was impressed.

"Thank you for seeing me, Menna," he said. Menna strode to him, stopping only a few inches away.

"I agreed to see you because long ago you did me a favor," she said. "What do you want, horro?"

"The world has changed," Famara said. "There

our forces outside this land that wish to make us their servants. To stop them we must fight together."

Menna smirked. "The Soninke and the Ihaaggaren have hated each other for centuries. You ask for too much in such a short time."

"Old enemies must become new friends if either are to continue to exist," Famara said.

Menna did not answer.

Famara tilted his head. "What do you want?"

Menna smiled. "Timbuktu."

Art by Anna Christenson.
http://freshpaint.deviantart.com/

THE ART & ARTIST

THE BOOK

Published with the assistance of BePublished.Org, **From My Facebook Friends** is Mylia Tiye Mal Jaza's 19th published book and it presents snapshots of social media posts the author's friends made on Facebook that invoked emotion and incited thought.

Compiled with the hope of showing everyone that what is placed in the public domain even through social media is accessible (and able to be redistributed at will) by the general public, Jaza hopes **From My**

Facebook Friends will inspire herself, friends and associates to always seek to encourage others and to think thrice about the emotions and reactions words shared incite.

Jaza says she also hopes **From My Facebook Friends** will remind creatives to not release poetry / stories / drawings / music / etc., online if the work hasn't previously been published and a copyright established.

Muhammad Asad of Pakistan has more than five years of experience designing book covers. One who believes, "creativity is the way of bringing out unorthodox innovations," his specializations are image composting, web designer/developer, photo retouching, flyers, posters, book covers, and many other designs.

In addition to **<u>Unspoken Truth of Jarvis Jones</u>**, Muhammad has lent his design expertise to a handful of other books published by BePublished.Org. He is fluent in Urdu and English, and enjoys spending time with his relatives and friends.

Mylia Tiye Mal Jaza (Mary "Mari" Michelle Jefferson) is a former Texas resident and Mississippi native presently residing in Illinois. She graduated from Jackson State University and the University of Texas at Dallas, and holds an honorary doctorate degree from Trinity Evangelical Christian University.

The entrepreneur, former professional model, and wedding officiant is also an award-winning journalist who gives back to the communities in which she lives and conducts business by mentoring teens, cleaning highways, feeding the homeless, providing gifts to nursing home residents, organizing community art exhibits and music festivals, and conducting school supplies drives for youth.

Also known as Sun Child Wind Spirit, Jaza (aka Goddess Sage) is a vocalist who has performed alongside international artists and at popular venues. She also helps writers with an array of editorial and business services including self-publishing and promotions training through BePublished.Org.

Not counting the March 2017 release of **From My Facebook Friends**, three of Mylia's 19 published books were works she published that were written by ancestors and relatives of hers – The Facts Of Reconstruction *by John R. Lynch*, The Old Negro And The New Negro *by T. Leroy Jefferson, M.D.*, and Mother's Mantras *by Susie W. Jefferson*.

In addition to **From My Facebook Friends**, Mylia's other 16 books were original works she created that ranged in content from poetry and prose to film and television scripts: Life Is Beautiful: La Vita E Bella, Life Is Beautiful: La Vita Es Hermosa, Seen In Other Words, Plea For Peace, All For Show,

<u>Scientific Evidence God Exists</u>, <u>Elegies Of A Goddess</u>, <u>AND</u>, <u>Get Off Your Packages</u>, <u>My Plan For Every Bully</u>, <u>Stop & Tie Your Shoes</u>, <u>P.E.N.I.S.</u>, <u>When The Quarterback Got Cut</u>, <u>FOOLISH OF ME: Addressing Love Unappreciated</u>, and <u>Amour Noir.</u>

MarryUsNow.us   **BePublished.org**

Order Books By Mylia Jaza & Family

Thank you for your support.

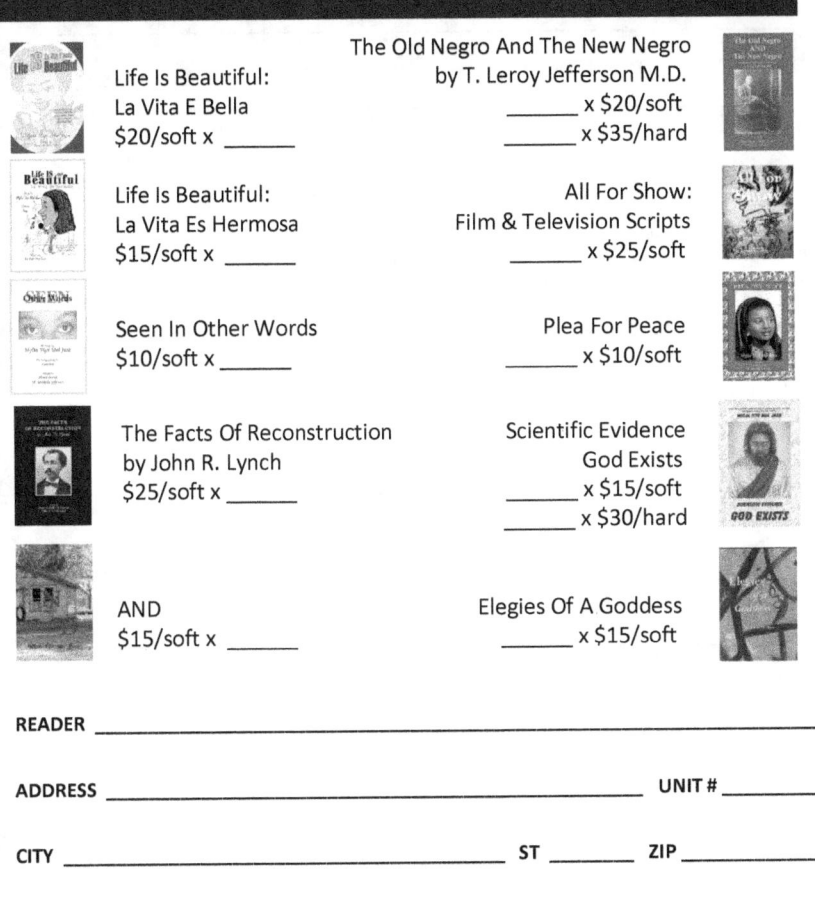

Life Is Beautiful:
La Vita E Bella
$20/soft x _____

The Old Negro And The New Negro
by T. Leroy Jefferson M.D.
_____ x $20/soft
_____ x $35/hard

Life Is Beautiful:
La Vita Es Hermosa
$15/soft x _____

All For Show:
Film & Television Scripts
_____ x $25/soft

Seen In Other Words
$10/soft x _____

Plea For Peace
_____ x $10/soft

The Facts Of Reconstruction
by John R. Lynch
$25/soft x _____

Scientific Evidence
God Exists
_____ x $15/soft
_____ x $30/hard

AND
$15/soft x _____

Elegies Of A Goddess
_____ x $15/soft

READER _____

ADDRESS _____ UNIT # _____

CITY _____ ST _____ ZIP _____

EMAIL _____ COUNTY _____ COUNTRY _____

Remit Payment For Selected Books + Form + $5 s/h To:

Mary M. Jefferson
P.O. Box 8324
Jackson, MS 39284

Please allow three (3) weeks minimum delivery to
allow for order processing, autographing of books, and shipment
to your address provided above.

Which Book(s) Autographed Using Which Individual(s) Name(s):

_____

_____

_____

_____

Your Thoughts About Recipient(s):

_____

_____

_____

_____

Personal Message From You To Author(s):

_____

_____

_____

_____

_____

_____

_____

Other Books By Mylia Jaza & Family

Thank you for your support.

 Children's Book
The Animals *by Isaiah Walls Palmer*
$25/soft x _____

Cat's Colors *by Kelvin T. Johnson*
Children's Book
_____ x $25/soft

 The Artistic Sketch Of Me
by Latisha A. Jefferson
$20/soft x _____

My Plan For Every Bully
Children's Book
_____ x $25/soft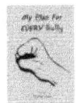

 Stop And Tie Your Shoes
$20/soft x _____

Get Off Your Packages
_____ x $20/soft

 P.E.N.I.S.
$20/soft x _____

When The Quarterback Got Cut
_____ x $20/soft

 Mother's Mantras
by Susie W. Jefferson
$20/soft x _____

Foolish of Me:
Addressing Love Unappreciated
_____ x $20/soft

READER _____

ADDRESS _____ UNIT # _____

CITY _____ ST _____ ZIP _____

EMAIL _____ COUNTY _____ COUNTRY _____

Remit Payment For Selected Books + Form + $5 s/h To:
Mary M. Jefferson
P.O. Box 8324
Jackson, MS 39284

Please allow three (3) weeks minimum delivery to allow for order processing, autographing of books, and shipment to your address provided to us above.

Which Book(s) Autographed Using Which Individual(s) Name(s):

_____

_____

_____

_____

Your Thoughts About Recipient(s):

_____

_____

_____

_____

Personal Message From You To Author(s):

_____

_____

_____

_____

_____

_____

_____

Other Books By Mylia Jaza & Family

Thank you for your support.

Amour Noir
$20/soft x _____

From My Facebook Friends
_____ x $15/soft

Sweet Mary:
Infused Food & Beverage Offering
$25/soft x _____

Niggas & Flies
_____ x $15/soft

READER _____

ADDRESS _____ UNIT # _____

CITY _____ ST _____ ZIP _____

EMAIL _____ COUNTY _____ COUNTRY _____

Remit Payment For Selected Books + Form + $5 s/h To:
Mary M. Jefferson
P.O. Box 8324
Jackson, MS 39284

Please allow three (3) weeks minimum delivery to allow for order processing, autographing of books, and shipment to your address provided to us above.

Which Book(s) Autographed Using Which Individual(s) Name(s):

_____

_____

_____

_____

Your Thoughts About Recipient(s):

_____

_____

_____

_____

Personal Message From You To Author(s):

_____

_____

_____

_____

_____

_____

_____